copyright © 2023
by
Alex Ayuli
Copyright throughout the world

A Blue Logic Publication

No parts of this book may be reproduced or transmitted in whole or part, in any form, without permission from the publisher

ISBN 978-1-088-25722-7

Preface

2020 was an historic year. It was the year of the Pandemic when the world was effectively shut down as we, the human species, waited out the rise and fall of a deadly global virus.

It was also a year of intense introspection for me personally. A year when I began looking 'inwards' as never before, – questioning everything. A year in which I spent a considerable amount of 'time' abiding in the wordless state of presence the Teacher has called Uncreated Light. It led to some life altering discoveries, insights, and experiences that I wanted to share with other students that I held a deep respect and admiration for. And so began my quest to initiate, co-ordinate, and collaborate on a discussion of the ancient, perennial questions: *Who am I? and, What is Presence?*

Three fellow students immediately came to mind - Girard Haven, John Craig, and Hugh Lusted. And I was incredibly fortunate that they were able to generously set aside the time to participate. I chose Hugh, John, and Girard primarily because of their profound Being, but also because of Girard and Hugh's prodigious intellectual capabilities, and John's no lesser intellect, but one that I intuited would have a more emotional sensibility, closer to my own. As John is a poet, I felt his way of seeing would be oriented in a slightly different direction, and be perhaps more in tune with how I thought about things as a musician, and I wanted to capture some of this in what was discussed.

To my mind, the four of us turned out to be a perfect combination, but I'll leave that for you, the reader, to decide.

Alex Ayuli, Sacramento CA

--o--

Our gathering produced a remarkable symposium, both poignantly personal and humbly profound, in which four older students shared their recent realizations about the limits of lower centers and the wonder of higher centers. Each of the participants addressed the question of identity and the experience of Presence from a different angle. Yet there were no contradictions. The understandings of each allowed room for those of all the others, and the resulting unity could be a verification of the effects of long work in a Conscious School.

John Craig, Apollo, CA

Acknowledgements

To our dear Teacher, without whom none of this would be possible. To the Absolute, and C Influence, without whom nothing would be possible.

Sunday 12/6/2020

Attendees: Girard Haven, Hugh Lusted, John Craig, Alex Ayuli.

Session begins

Alex: So, there are two initial directives that I have for this experiment. The two would be for us to not assume anything and to question everything: If something is said that generates a question, then just ask that question. So that we can be as open as possible about this. This opening topic is something I began thinking about from a different point of view, over this past summer: *Who am I? And what is presence?* And even this morning when I was looking over my notes, I had another thought that maybe it would be more appropriate to say; *Who is I?*

I would like to keep the format open, if at any time anyone has any questions or angles, please just interject so we can keep this thing fluid. If this works, I'm hoping that over time, we can get to a level of trust that we can feel free to say anything as long as it's trying to get at the truth, I believe the radical truth of who or what we are...

Let's start with my definition of who I am, and then I invite everyone to contribute whatever it is you feel about the subject. I want to start with a definition of what I considered to be me until recently. As a child there were many occasions where I remember looking out of my eyes from the point of view of an observer. And this point of view never really went away. But what I saw was that most of the time it receded into the background of my life, and then particularly after joining the school it began to come more and more into the foreground. I think this is the influence of Robert's teaching. He is so focused on being present, and the observer, that the longer you're in the school, the more you absorb, the more it comes into the foreground. But it was something that I realized was always there, and at different times in my life, even before the school, there would be a very strong feeling of presence. A certain shock would happen, and that (presence) would be there. So that was my 'ground zero' for a long time, being this observer, but now I've discovered something else...

One of the things about this state is that it hasn't changed. It doesn't seem to know any more than when I was a young child. It doesn't seem to have any kind of opinion, or information... it just seems to 'be', and it's almost as if, in relation to it, my life as Alex never existed. It doesn't seem to have taken anything from the role of Alex. It is completely separate. And this summer, I came to a completely different point of view about what that is, and I'll come back to that later...

And then, what is presence? A few weeks before I joined the school, I remember Rodney Collin saying in *Theory of Celestial Influence* that the first time you hear about self-remembering, or the first time you read those words, in that very moment you self-remember. And I remember at the time I was sitting in front of a large plate glass window, it was dark on the other side of the window, and I read that line and looked up. And I saw myself looking at a reflection of myself, looking back at me.

It was really powerful. It was an addition to being an observer. And the reflection in the window kind of triggered an intuition – something that was not fully formed, that was contributing to the power of that moment. It was an immediate verification of the truth of what Collin had said, that those words would trigger the state. I didn't understand this at the time, but later I realized it also verified Rodney Collin's idea of self-remembering being not just the observer and the observed, but the idea that there's a third element in the picture that he equated to higher forces or God.

And this third element was what turned divided attention into self-remembering. As I said, I did not realize this at the time, it was something that came back to me much later. So as profound as that moment was for me, I didn't stop to contemplate what had happened. It registered that I was present, I realized that I was reading something that had the truth, that these ideas were really important, and then I turned back to the book and continued to read.

And then soon after, I joined the school and began the work in earnest.

And it wasn't until this past summer that I reflected back on that moment with the new understanding that I think I have. What I see now is that, that moment was a very powerful rendering of what I understand as objective consciousness. From that, what I understand now, which relates back to what I said about the observer; presence, having no connection to the role, what I understand now is that Alex, the student, is a projected reflection in the mind. He is a mental image, and in that sense, doesn't have any objective reality.

So, I'm going to stop here for now and I'd really love to hear your thoughts, experiences, or whatever it is you've been thinking about when it comes to considering the questions; *What is presence? Who am I?*

Hugh: One thought that comes to mind is having the experience recently, when presence is here, it incorporates divided attention. And in a sense, it took me a while to notice that. And then it completely makes sense why that is a starting point: By dividing attention, it's possible as Ouspensky said, to get the state going, but what's really delightful is being present then that comes with the package, that's wonderful.

Alex: Do you think about what it is that's present?

Hugh: No. These days when an I comes, it's a reminder just to be present. I don't think about it. I would rather have the state than any thoughts.

Girard: One understanding that I've been developing more fully in the past year or so is that everything we say about it is an angle. And the word 'angle' is literally true. I now look at it as one of the brilliant ideas in our school because, as explained by Ouspensky and Collin, the world of presence, the world of higher centers is six dimensional.

We live in a four-dimensional world, so there are things that Influence C are aware of, and thoughts or experiences that they are able to have, which we are literally unable to have because we don't have the equipment. So, everything is a translation into four dimensions, which is a view from our world of a higher world. Just the way a drawing on paper of a three-dimensional object is one angle. And you take the same object and turn it, and you get a different view. It's the same object but it depends on the angle. And everything has angles.

So, if you ask me most of these questions my answer tends to be, well, yes you could think of it that way. I don't always bother to. And this is one of the things I've encountered; I've been leading many online meetings so far this year, I think there's been twenty in the last six months, and it's one of those things I always try to mention: don't worry about the definitions. They're able to give some direction of where we are going, and they're also a way for the four lower centers to deal with the experience of something they're not capable of.

And suddenly this happens to them. And it can be very confusing. That's why Gurdjieff says if you were just suddenly to awaken, you would go mad. And it's true. The analogy I use is; we have six dogs in the house, and it's like if I tried to read Shakespeare to my dogs, they don't understand that at all. And yet Robert lives in a world, that compared to ours, our world is very closely analogous to the world of a dog compared to his.

So, I always try to then come back to the simple answer of; try to be here now. Whatever I call it, whatever happens to make the machine happy with the idea at the time, it just makes the effort. So, if you were to ask me what I consider to be myself, I can give you various angles, none of which are good explanations at all.

So that's where I am currently; there is something, and it is like having a different center beyond the four we are familiar with, somehow you are experiencing things in a different way and any attempt to explain them by the four lower centers will be unsatisfactory because they are incapable of experiencing them.

Alex: I agree fully with that; that the intellect tries to articulate for itself, tries to explain the experience by saying; well, that must have been this, for instance, and like you say, it's never satisfactory. But it's not necessarily useless, otherwise we would have no books on the subject. We would have no Gurdjieff and Ouspensky. They wrote something down using their centers, that they left to us and I find now that, certainly Gurdjieff pointed to a lot of things without fully articulating them, and that was because he couldn't, but he could at least point, and that's the best that we can do. Just to point. Just to try to find a way of conveying something that's so hard to do.

I guess that's why you have art, and music. People are trying to convey something that feels real or true and they don't have another way to express it. Poetry is another very good example of that.

John, I know you're very interested in poetry, which is partly why I wanted you to be on the discussion because perhaps there are angles in poetry that resonate with you that maybe you've experienced. I know, for example, that Rumi is one of the people using poetry and words, and somehow he manages to express the inexpressible.

John: Well, I was struck by your opening, Alex, about the first time you came across the phrase, self-remembering, because I had a similar experience in the summer of 1980 in the North Hollywood Library, the first time I came across the word self-remembering. It was in a book on Eastern yogis which made a very slight, one line reference to Gurdjieff. It hurled me into a higher state that lasted for about three days and sent me looking much more assiduously for a school.

But that state was like a hallucinogenic state but without the impurities of a state that is drug induced. And it was clear as it was going on that for me to actually experience that state to its maximum, I -- what I considered to be I at the time -- had to be completely passive and just let it take its course.

And forty years later I've come to the conclusion that anything John Craig has to say about all of this is pretty limited and inarticulate. John Craig is like a character in a video game. I don't know who has the controls and is moving the images around, and what the purpose is other than its entertainment, but I am completely sure at this point that John Craig, and Girard Haven, and all of us are illusions in our distension. That what exists is one thing, the totality.

One thing exists and as we get more and more distant from it -- now distance is actually a met- aphor here, not a physical property -- as we get more and more distant from it, we become more distinct in being illusions. And as we come closer and closer to the truth, we exist less and less as individual beings.

So, anything that comes to John Craig, the individual being, I know to be an illusion. I still get identified with it, still get caught up in it, snagged by it, but ultimately, it's an illusion. And I'll be glad to get to the other side. As for the poetry, for me, poetry is a practice. The state writes the poem. I have no idea what's going to get written when I sit down to write. The best I can do with what has been written is correct the grammar and syntax a little bit and polish it up. But the state writes the poem, and all I do is write it down.

Alex: Yes, that's my experience as a musician, I'm not writing the songs, they're coming through, let's say. They come through and you try to manage the process. You choose an instrument that might convey something, or you look for a sound, and so on. And I think when you really study your life, let's say you're having a conversation with your wife or a friend, when I look at that now, I see it is completely spontaneous.

Like right now, I've no idea what I'm going to say next, it's completely spontaneous. A poem may have a certain direction or a certain feeling, but an ordinary conversation also comes from the same place. It's all coming from spontaneity, which I think is beyond the four lower centers, which are, as you say, they're illusory at worst and at best they're a tool, or a way for something to be expressed.

I side more and more with you that there's an illusory aspect to all this. And when you say, John Craig, and Girard, and Hugh, and Alex, you can't leave out anything else; you have to include the world, even the universe if you're thinking on that scale. There's something that you said that perfectly encapsulates what I was thinking. I want to share with you an image, it's a funny equation. It's when you said that 'I' has to be one thing.

So, it can't be simply my I or your I, it has to be some kind of Universal I expressing itself infinitely throughout the universe.

$$I = 1$$

Then I began playing around with numbers and came up with another formulation that tries to explain what we see in our Universe. If you divide one by zero you get Infinity.

$$1 \div 0 = \infty$$

This was just an intuition but then the intellectual center tried to formulate it in this way. I don't know if it's correct but the intuition pointed to the idea that out of one or unity divided by zero or nothingness you get everything.

That somehow expresses to me the Gurdjieff Ray of Creation, which I think of now as a ray of consciousness. In which everything is conscious, and its not a ray because it's infinite. Perhaps we only perceive it as a ray. But it's infinite and conscious at every point.

Gurdjieff said that there were different densities of what he called hydrogens, but maybe it's actually densities of consciousness. So, consciousness can be as dense as a rock --- World 768 -- or as fine as the Will of the Absolute -- World 1.

But the paradox in this is that a rock can be made out of consciousness, and somehow there's this idea of the universe being an illusion. And I just sit there in the middle and try to be at peace with the fact that there's a paradox there which certainly the lower centers will never get to understand, but perhaps through intuition, the higher centers will know what this is about and communicate that.

I'm a great believer in intuition as being how the higher centers manifest through the machine. I've been having a flood of insights, and there have been shocks this past summer that have put me onto a new track which I'm finding very fruitful. I'm sure that we all are finding a way of working with whatever new thing comes into our consciousness and I'm interested in exploring whatever that is for each of us.

--o--

Girard: Something that has been useful for me is an angle in *In Search of the Miraculous,* in Chapter 8, where Ouspensky talks about dividing oneself, making a distinction, in my case, between Girard and I. And it has become very clear to me that Girard goes through a very human life of his own and sometimes I am there and sometimes I am not. But if Robert's right that I is outside of time then you can't really talk about being there at times and not there at others because time is not the same for I.

But just to have that sense of the division between the two. And it's a better angle for explaining my current experience, whereas a few years ago it seemed a more theoretical idea. Now, it seems like I am tending to view my experience in the school from that point of view and it seems to fit.

Alex: I wanted to ask a question, Girard, to clarify because I remember reading that also and it was very useful for me as well. So, when you do that, do you align yourself, your identity with I and not with Girard?

Girard: Alex, to be honest I have to say I find that question irrelevant, like it just doesn't fit. I don't know, I don't have any sense of myself as something, there are just these various experiences. I don't know, that's not an angle I'm able to use right now. I look at that angle and it doesn't seem to fit. Doesn't help explain something. Since they are all, in my opinion, varied angles, and you just try to find the one in the moment or in a particular time period that seems to help the four centers help Girard interpret what is happening. I am very hesitant that we'd be talking about Girard under the influence of something higher and I am hesitant to put labels on it because that limits more than it clarifies.

John: I like the idea of dividing x and y. If John Craig is the y, then the thing that's most evident about John Craig is that everything comes from his four lower centers, and I use the word 'mind' as a shorthand for that. And I use the phrase 'above mind' for something that is not that. And that distinction -- mind and above mind -- works pretty well. And I agree with Girard; I, is just a cursor, a line of continuum that measures in any given moment, how much of a distinct illusion you are. If you get up the ray of creation far enough, past the lower centers, past mind, another word that seems to articulate the inclusiveness of that territory is 'God'. 'I' is becoming more and more a feeble tool as time goes on. And I don't understand how Robert uses it.

Alex: Real I. What I like about the word is that it's so simple. But what I try to do with it is depersonalize it. So, the I could be God, it could be the Absolute. By trying to depersonalize it, maybe it comes back to its true meaning; that I is not referring to a person. And it comes back to the idea of the Absolute in the sense of what an Absolute implies: that there is nothing else. So only the Absolute can be I. And that's how Everything can be I, and also Nothing can be I.

I also understand that these are just concepts, notions in the intellectual center. And so, they're useful as handholds, but then you have to let them go, so you can go up to the next level and then look for the next one. This is not from the intellectual center, this is all coming from intuition, that I think comes from the higher centers. Having the division that Girard has -- between Girard and 'I' -- is paramount for all of us. But there may not be any real distance between them.

If I is the source of everything, and it's projecting, then those projections are still I, they're coming from the source so they have what we could call a relative reality. Which is another paradox: the illusion is relatively real. We're here existing, living, we're real but I also understand fully that it's also an illusion. It's a struggle to get this out, words are such blunt instruments but they're all that we have. Robert uses words to try to convey these impossible things and we just have to deal with that. They're all that we have....

(problems with audio)

Girard: Maybe Influence C are playing with the audio.

Hugh: Right. That's what I thought. It's part of the experience... I wanted to share an experience of an illusion. I recently had a dream which took place in some family's living room, I didn't recognize any of the people. Suddenly some awareness woke up in the dream and started intentionally looking around the room. The observer was aware of looking intentionally. Looked at the pictures on the walls, the furniture, and the people. In particular there were two children, and I had prolonged eye contact with a little girl who appeared to be six or seven years old.

When I woke to 2nd state, I realized it was an example of being awake in an illusory setting and the intentionality of looking around the room was striking. Specifically, the observer could choose what to look at and for how long. Emotionally it felt the same as intentionally looking around the room right now. So, when I woke up, it really made me think about the world of illusion.

That, that experience was real, the observer had no sense of I at all, it just simply was observing and also there was no thought that that was an illusion. It was as real in the dream as sitting here now. It created the third state and it made me think about the nature of illusion and every day second state life, so I thought I'd share that since we're talking about illusions.

Alex: Yes, that's beautiful, I've had very similar dreams. I remember having a dinner with Dorian in the Galleria, downstairs and we were talking along those lines and I related a very recent dream at that time, and I said it was as real as this (the dinner), how do we know this isn't a dream? And the question just sat there for a while. The illusion is hyper real. It has infinite detail.

Hugh: Yes.

Girard: You have to remember that the idea of something being an illusion is an illusion itself. So, if you think like that then it makes the whole idea meaningless. Recently that has been much more my direction because then you are left with nothing except to be present, whatever that means in the moment. All the explanations come to nothing. I developed what for me was a very satisfactory mathematical explanation. I mention it quickly because I know Hugh will be able to follow it, I don't know how much mathematics the rest of you have.

Alex: Not much.

Hugh: Maybe a little.

Girard: Well, playing around for several years with the idea of infinity and many, many dimensions and such things did a good job of making my ordinary experience seem irrelevant, but then Robert says the angels can move faster than the speed of light to get around the universe. The mathematical equations set the speed of light as a limit. They're not actually saying that you can't go faster than the speed of light, what they say is if there are bodies moving relative to each other, at faster than the speed of light, the effect would be one of them would measure the others not with numbers we are used to, but that mass, time, and space would all be measured by what we call imaginary numbers.

Mathematically, imaginary numbers are for dealing with numbers like the square root of a minus one, which means the square root of any negative number. So, what do you do with them? Nothing.

Anyway, for a long time mathematicians thought that way. Then one day one of them said, *Let's pretend there is something we can measure with this square root of a negative one if we simply call it 'i'"*. And that's what they did. The 'i' suddenly became the "i" for an imaginary number, and mathematicians started working out very complete theories about it.

So, what this could mean is that the angels or conscious beings live in a space which can be measured with imaginary numbers. But I don't have any idea what that means. It is totally incomprehensible to me, existing on an entirely different plane from anything else.

One of the interesting things about this, -- and strangely enough I started playing with this idea when I was in college -- is that I said to myself, *Well, let's just assume that things can move faster than the speed of light* and I took the basic Newtonian rules of the physics for the world we live in and then said, *Well, if these things moving faster than the speed of light are imaginary, what happens?*

What's interesting is that 'force' turns out to be real and imaginary at the same time. And that explains how higher forces exert influence C on us in this world. Even existing in a world measured by imaginary numbers like the square root of minus one, they can still produce real effects on us.

I thought to myself that is so nice and I just stopped there at that point and didn't do any more thinking about it. And what it had done was make it all so totally incomprehensible to me that I completely dropped all the I's I would ever have about explaining higher states, or what it is or anything else I have experienced over the last year or two, and simply be at peace about it.

Beyond that, it really is literally incomprehensible, and I don't waste my time any more trying to comprehend it, and I find that very satisfying.

So, that's why with all these questions right now, they're kind of fun to play with intellectually, but I'm not really interested in that anymore, and everything is really just about, alright, be here. I don't know what all this stuff is about. Because it's completely incomprehensible. Which is also very exciting, that one enters a new world that is so extreme that one can't even count. Like I know what an i.apple is but not what an 'I' apple is. Makes no sense. Wonderful!

Alex: Yes, and I didn't know this at the time, when I first encountered those workbooks, that we were dealing with things that couldn't be comprehended by the intellectual center. There was always the idea that by the time I am done I'll understand all of this, but that's obviously not the case. What is reading the books doesn't understand the implications of what it is reading.

When you talk about an Absolute or Infinity, they're words that you understand, but I didn't fully see the implications of those words until very recently. The Absolute for me was just a name, it was a noun when in fact it's far more than that. The Absolute is, quite literally, everything. This is kind of what I was alluding to earlier.

Girard: I think you can be relatively confident that in a few years from now, what you understand now, will be like the word 'Absolute' was to you ten years ago. The lower self wants to think that something will know, and it thinks that what it knows now is an answer, and it's not. And that's what is nice about the idea that consciousness is a space that includes imaginary numbers. And that puts it so totally beyond any kind of imagination, that I was able to drop all thoughts.

So yes, there can be new words or symbols and one can play around with them like one divided by zero equals infinity, but beyond that there is a simple space of not knowing, and one can be absolutely content with not knowing.

Alex: There is something that you said that I want to talk about; when you said that you came to this calculation but you just could not think about it and so you just had to let it go. Is that correct Girard?

Girard: Think about it is not the right word; it was more like... comprehend it, or conceive of it, it was incomprehensible, unthinkable, unimaginable. It is those but it's much more. We can go back to the dog: A Shakespeare sonnet is simply inconceivable to a dog. Only we're not even that close to Higher Centers so the analogy is a little weak because dogs are much closer to our experience, or at least I think so. But it gives one an image. And dogs don't worry about the fact that they don't understand Shakespeare.

We have the ability to imagine, and it's both a danger but it's also a very, very powerful tool. We could not possibly awaken except that we imagine things can be other than they are. It's a gift that makes awakening possible but at the same time it is so powerful that its misuse is very dangerous.

Alex: This place of inconceivability is the place, I think, where the intellectual mind stops, and I think is the place where Higher Centers, or the Real 'I' starts. And so, the mind gets kind of blown in a way at that point. But that doesn't mean that the reality or the truth of whatever it was that seemed inconceivable is inaccessible. It's just not accessible to the mind.

John: That would be my sense of it also, Alex. That it's not accessible to the mind. The mind bounces around inside the brain case and is in jail so to speak. Like the business with the speed of light being a maximum and we can't go faster than the speed of light. The problem is the mind identifies things in specific locations that have to traverse distances, and that involves speed. In fact, the real problem is the identification with being a thing at a specific location.

The reason we can't see something reaching a point faster than the speed of light is because we don't have the fluidity to accept that we're already there. There is no distance, there is no speed, there are not two objects with a distance between them. There's only One Thing -- which we participate in relatively and if we participate in it at a certain level, or maybe, perfectly, we're here and there at the same time. It's the identification that gives us all the problems, especially the identification with our minds.

Alex: There's this idea that Robert often mentions: Because speed is in relation to travelling through space, you cannot ignore the aspect of time. And when Robert talks about being outside of time, when you think about what that means, it all becomes very flummoxing as well. It's another place where the mind breaks down. But there is some other way to access that understanding, and it's in higher centers.

My intuition about time, and it has to be the same with space, is that they don't actually exist either. They're just concepts, they're just ways for the body, the intellect to deal with what we're calling reality right now that seems to have time and space in it. What I saw about time was that we break it down into these three components; we have the future, the past and we have the present. But when you think about it; the future doesn't exist because it's not actually here yet, the past doesn't exist because we're not experiencing the past, but the present doesn't actually exist either, there is no present since it is always disappearing before you can even notice it.

So, there's no time. We can only ever say it's now. If someone was to ask, what time is it? I can always say now and be correct. But in fact, that doesn't really exist. So, being outside of time implies an understanding that time is just the way we think about things here. And if there's no time, there can be no space either. It's not just the intellect, it's our four lower centers, they bind us, they keep us in this place of not knowing what we are, where we are, what's going on. They're just interpreting things to make it easy for them to navigate this world.

But I'm sure we've all had that experience where we were outside of time, and time had a completely different flavor. When you go to sleep at night, and you dream, and in the dream maybe you're there for days and then you wake up and realize it's just been a couple of hours. And sometimes you don't even dream, you're just gone. You're in what they call the deep sleep, and there's nothing. You don't remember anything, you just know that you must have been there because you're still here when you open your eyes, so you must have been here while you were asleep. But you know nothing about it.

So, there's no time and no space in deep sleep. It's beyond the mind. I guess to awaken means to be beyond the mind. Not that the mind disappears but somehow there's an understanding of what is beyond it, that's informing the mind, maybe projecting into the mind.

John: We're identified with bodies, and if we're identified with bodies, we experience time and space. And it doesn't matter if it's a cellular body, or an astral body, or whatever kind of body theoretically comes after that, and until we're no longer identified with bodies, we're going to be experiencing time and space on some level.

Alex: Yes, I had similar thoughts about that. As long as there's a body there's a sense of self – something experiencing something.

Girard: There is the skin, inside it there's meat, there is a body, and there is something larger in which the body exists certainly, and this creates duality.

John: And it's downhill from there on!

Girard: We can explain it in many ways but since they're all equally unsatisfactory, I've given up.

--o--

Alex: Hugh, in your dream is there anything more you can tell us about that?

Hugh: Well, the most striking thing that I remember is that something woke up in that room and intentionally looked around. That to me was an unusual experience, and at the same time there was no thought or impression that it was a dream; that it was an illusion. So, it's as though the observer was just looking at that artificial situation. It had no identity, there was no sense of I, but there was a definite sense of being present. Of observing, and the surprising ability to look around and take in impressions. I guess that's what was striking about the dream.

Alex: Was that the reality of your dream? That you were able to do that.

Hugh: Yes, when I woke up, that was the surprising thing; first of all, to remember those details and particularly having eye contact with the children. Having control, having control in that room, whatever that room was. There was a definite feeling to that.

Alex: I suspect that the moment you would have had a thought, you would have been out of that dream. Somehow, for me, when I'm in a dream like that; a lucid dream? In all of my dreams there's never a thought. It's always feelings and actions. Whenever there's a thought, I wake up. Whenever I think I'm in a dream then I wake up out of it. There's a knowing that I'm in the dream, but there's no thought about it. Until I wake up. But having a dream like that, you have to question your reality, in this place, in this world, you have to question that.

Hugh: Right. Yes.

Alex: And I think that's what's been interesting for me this year. Really questioning reality. Even now, I'm present now, it's like being present in a dream. It's the same feeling. There's a certain kind of reality but there's a certain kind of unreality. But I'm not present out of the dream. Like you can be present in a dream, and then you awaken out of the dream and that dream disappears. It's gone and you realize that it never existed.

So, maybe that's the next step from this place that the higher centers are capable of. And of course, that's going to be incomprehensible to anything in time and space; to the mind it's going to be completely incomprehensible. That's about where I'm at with it. That whatever the awakening is, will be incomprehensible. But it won't necessarily be destructive. And I think that's partly because of our time in the school; these years and years and years and years of working on ourselves, that's been melting away that part that could have had a very terrible reaction.

If it had happened thirty or forty years ago it might have been very destructive, and you might think that you were going crazy. But I think we're slowly being tempered or molded, or that aspect is being sloughed off, just through time and doing the work. So that whatever comes next, we'll still be able to operate.

Robert operates in this world very well, so it's not that we have to go mad because of the awakening. But certainly, within the first five years, maybe we're not ready for that. I'm the youngest person in the school here and I'm thirty-one in the school. So, I think we might all be surprised by what we're capable of.

Robert was so surprised, he said, when he crystallized, his World Six came on and handled it. I asked him, was that a surprise? And he said yes it was because up until that point

World Twelve had done everything. He didn't even really know much about World Six and then suddenly in the crucial moment, that's what appeared and took care of that moment. So, as Ouspensky said, something will rise to the occasion.

John: If you don't buffer it.

Alex: When you say buffer, what do you mean, John?

John: Object to it, shrink from it, try to defend against it. Make some kind of motion from the lower self and the lower centers to thwart it.

Alex: Absolutely, although even that probably will end up being futile. It may delay things but certainly can't derail things at this point. But yes, the machine is designed to survive. That's its goal, is to survive and propagate in this world. I'm sure that's part of the calculation of awakening is that yes, there's something that objects, that doesn't want it.

John: Is afraid of it.

Alex: Yes. I wanted to ask Robert if there was any fear. Somehow the thought was surprise, but I wanted to ask if he was afraid. Because that's such a moment when you think about it. It's kind of a death, this crystallization. Something that had control will never have control again, since something else takes over. That thing that had control is dead. Not dead as in inert, but it is no longer in control.

Girard did you ever have any thoughts about Robert's crystallization, when his Real I came and stayed.

Girard: The way I think about it is, reading the works of other conscious beings, it does not seem like they all had such a dramatic moment. So apparently it doesn't always happen that way, or it's not always experienced that way -- as a moment of crystallization.

I think that way intentionally because it neutralizes the I's of the lower self about that experience, and about the fact that I have never had anything even vaguely similar.

So, I can tell myself, *Oh yes, but how many conscious beings have you heard about with stories like that?* Something happened for him, some threshold was crossed. And it may have been very much like you described, but it doesn't mean that I will experience it that way. But it is hard not to have the lower self think about it. For instance, if the experience is out of time, I find that useful because I don't have any idea what out of time means except in a very theoretical way.

I have lived my whole life in time. There are a lot of things like that -- like the idea of a visitation of the Absolute: Now frankly I can't work with that, I don't have any idea what that would mean. What I would say is that it's clear that something very profound happened to Robert, and the way I look at it, that is the best way he can explain it with the tools he has -- with his machine and his vocabulary, he tries to talk about it.

He had some kind of profound experience and that's the best way he can describe it. But I don't know what it means, and I don't worry about it. I just say, *Yes, well, something happened!* If someone said, well suppose it's all his imagination? I'd say, yes, that could be. This is actually one of the I's I use to help neutralize the lower self: Suppose he is in imagination? Then I say to myself, *Well, alright maybe it's imagination.* I know my imagination, this world I imagine myself in has strange deformations and machinations. So, yes, I'll trade my imagination for his.

And of course, there's the possibility that what he is experiencing is not imagination, and that would be even better. So, I'll go his way and not be concerned about it because I can't lose. I'll either have a better life and then die, or I wake up. I'm going to die anyway so I might as well have the better life until then.

Alex: Yes, I fully concur with that. It's much better to be present than to be asleep. In fact, for me lately, being asleep, and it is mostly identification these days, but to not be there is something I experience much more profoundly; that Oh, there was no one there. I was driving for ten minutes and there was absolutely no one there. That's the feeling I have when I return; that there is nothing there, it was just mechanisms, habits operating. And then I'm back.

It's so much more validating to be there. I don't know how I got through it before. I don't know if the feeling of not being there was ever as strong as this. There was the personality and the habits, the ego was so taken for granted that I just assumed I was there, but now with those things severely weakened, it's quite obvious that there's no one there. Nothing there, but it can still drive a car and get home...

--o--

Alex: As unusual as it is, and it's not over yet, did this year make you look more deeply at things? To me, our mortality was so evident everywhere, it was so in your face, I turned inwards on it. It made me question; it made me look inwards much more than in other years. I wondered if it had the same effect on you all.

John: It was massively inconvenient, but I can't say I've been suffering. I'm retired and stay at home, and there really isn't a whole lot of difference in what I've been asked to do by the government and what I would normally be doing anyway. But it feels quite oppressive. Getting older into it and realizing that some measure of the oppression this year is probably going to continue for as long as I remain alive is something I haven't quite confronted yet.

Alex: I think maybe because I'm in life much more, and there are people out there that have been impacted by all of this. I work for a school district and they're all about this. It's been top of mind. There are emails every day and meetings, so it's had a larger impact. But it's been positive in the sense that I've thought more deeply about things. I've stopped taking many things for granted, or I've stopped making so many assumptions and begun to look into things more deeply and it's been very helpful. Because we take so much for granted, we assume so much. I didn't realize how much was being assumed.

John: I really miss hugging people.

Girard: Yes. And having dinners with them. Being something besides images on a computer screen.

Alex: It's gotten to the point where if I see something from last year, I'm thinking, why aren't those guys wearing masks? Then I remember, oh that's right, the virus wasn't there last year. But somehow, it's become conditioning. I'm thinking, will we get over this mask thing? When the vaccine is out there and everyone's vaccinated, will we still be nervous? Will we still be thinking about masks? Will we still have that sense of mortality that we have now?...

So, we've been speaking for nearly ninety minutes. How does everyone feel? Do we like this? Should we do this again at some other point? Do you want to keep going, or take a break, or stop? How does everyone feel about what we have?

Hugh: One thought here is just the practicality of si-do's I've left outside. I was just thinking about the one hour of light left. So, for me ninety minutes has been extraordinary, I didn't think we would go this long. It's been quite engaging.

Alex: Yes, I'm very happy that we did this. It's gone by fast and didn't feel like we were dragging on. Do you feel like it's something we should pursue? If, in a few weeks, anyone has something that comes up that they want to talk about, should we do another one of these?

John: I think we've set a pretty high bar. We've managed to determine that we are illusory creatures in the universe and it's hard to talk about little problems after this; a toothache or an immigration appointment, or whatever, kind of shrinks into nothingness, but yes, it's delightful just to get together on any terms that we can during these circumstances.

Alex: If any insights pop into your mind, or maybe you have another dream, Hugh, that you want to talk about. I just feel like it's nice if there's a space for things like this, a little bit more personal and more informal, but still going deeply into something, still rigorous as much as we can make it. I'd be very happy to do another one... Well, let's wrap it up then and I really thank you all for your contribution to this. It's been a wonderful experience. I'm looking forward to transcribing this, looking at what we have, and putting something together that you can read. And then we can talk about whether we want to do more or if this is it. I like the idea that people with long experience in the school, share some of that being and knowledge in a way that is less formalized, more of a conversation than a meeting.

John: Thanks for instigating it all, Alex.

Alex: Thanks, I appreciate you all for taking the time out of your day to do this.

Session Ends

www.ingramcontent.com/pod-product-compliance
Lightning Source LLC
Chambersburg PA
CBHW030458010526
44118CB00011B/1004